The Usborne
First Atlas

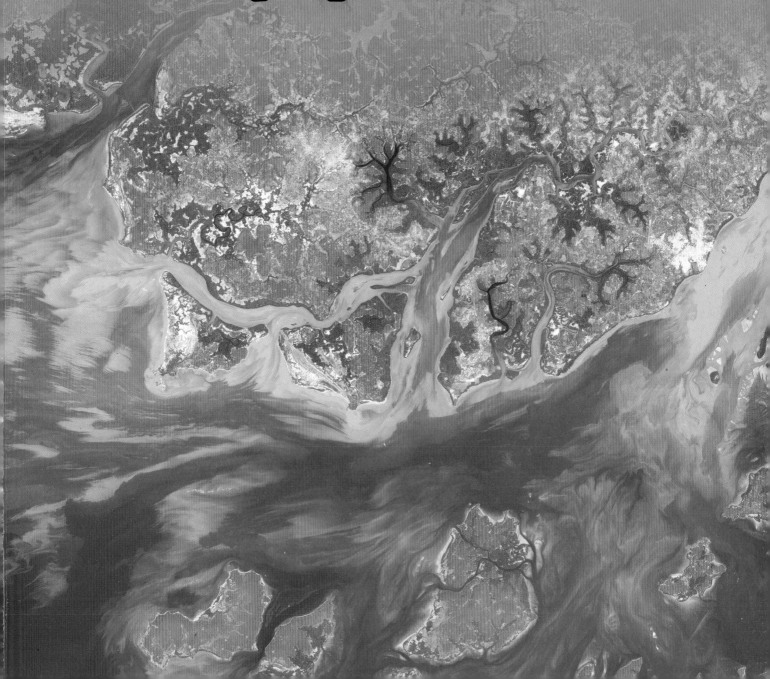

Title page: A satellite image showing rivers joining the sea, along the coast of
Guinea-Bissau in west Africa. The red parts are land and the blue parts are water.
This page: These mountains and glaciers are on the island of Svalbard, which belongs
to Norway. The island is far inside the Arctic Circle and it's very cold there.

The Usborne
First Atlas

Elizabeth Dalby

Designed by Laura Hammonds,
Candice Whatmore and Ruth Russell

Digital imagery by Keith Furnival

Edited by Kirsteen Rogers

Cover design: Steve Moncrieff

Consultant: John Davidson

Cartography: European Map Graphics Ltd

Consultant cartographic editor: Craig Asquith

Usborne Quicklinks

The Usborne Quicklinks Website is packed with links to the best websites on the internet. To find links for this book, go to:

www.usborne-quicklinks.com
and enter the keywords "first atlas"

You'll find links to websites where you can:
- Zoom into satellite images of Earth
- Take a photo tour of the Amazon Rainforest
- See the view from the top of Mount Everest
- Find out about the everyday lives of people around the world
- Try map games, puzzles and activities

Internet safety guidelines
When using the internet please follow the internet safety guidelines displayed on the Usborne Quicklinks Website.

The recommended websites in Usborne Quicklinks are regularly reviewed and updated, but Usborne Publishing Ltd is not responsible for the content or availability of any website other than its own. We recommend that children are supervised while using the internet.

Contents

These brightly painted houses are in Buenos Aires, the capital city of Argentina in South America.

About maps

An atlas is a collection of maps. Maps are pictures of areas, seen from above. They show places much smaller than they really are. Some maps show the whole world, and some show much smaller areas, like cities or streets.

What will you see on a map?

Maps should be easy to understand. Different kinds of shading and symbols help show what a place is like. A key explains what they all mean.

The size of a map compared with the real-life area it shows is called its scale. Some maps have a line called a scale bar that shows you the real distances between places on the map.

Which way is up?

The Earth doesn't really have a top and a bottom. Maps are often drawn with north at the top, though, to make them easier for everyone to understand.

Rio Grande

Mississippi

Gulf of Mexico

Central America

Cuba

Caribbean Sea

Guiana Highlands

Amazon

Amazon Rainforest

SOUTH AMERICA

Andes

Atacama Desert

Pampas

Patagonia

Cape Horn

Key to South and Central America map

- Forest
- Desert
- Grassland
- Mountain
- Crops

This map shows what the land in South and Central America is like.

Scale
Scale bar —
0km   2,000km
0 miles   1,240 miles

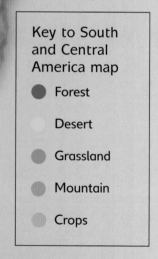

This compass symbol shows which way is north (N), south (S), east (E) and west (W).

Sea and land

More than two-thirds of the Earth is covered in salty water – the seas and oceans. Maps usually show water in blue.

The rest of the Earth is covered in land. Maps sometimes shade the land as it would look from above. Grasslands are often green and deserts can be sandy brown or yellow.

An island is land with water all around it. This is one of the Solomon Islands, in the Pacific Ocean.

Countries and continents

The land is divided into seven huge areas called continents, which are split into smaller areas called countries. Each country is run by a government and has its own laws. Some large countries are further divided into states, to make them easier to run.

Internet links

For links to websites where you can zoom into satellite images of the Earth, go to **www.usborne-quicklinks.com**

This is the continent of North America. It is a large area of land and islands.

North America is divided into countries, including Canada, the USA and Mexico.

The USA is divided into 50 different states. Each state can make its own laws.

Information from maps

Maps can show different things about the same area. Some maps show where countries and cities are. Some show what the land looks like or what kinds of plants grow there.

Political maps show countries and place names. The lines between countries are called borders or boundaries.

Physical maps show what the land looks like. They show features like mountains, lakes and rivers.

Thematic maps show other information, such as what the land is used for, or how many people live there.

Weather and wildlife

Different parts of the world have their own weather patterns, plants and wildlife. These areas are called biomes. Deserts, grasslands and rainforests are biomes. They can all be shown on a thematic map.

These cacti live in the desert, where it hardly ever rains. They store water in their stems.

Internet links

For links to websites where you can find map games and puzzles, go to **www.usborne-quicklinks.com**

How many people?

The people who live in an area are its population. Maps can be used to show which parts of an area are crowded, and which parts have very few people living in them.

This map of North America shows the areas where most people live.

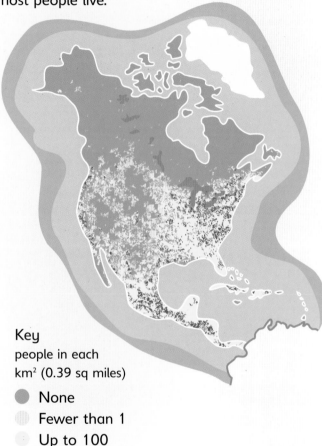

Key
people in each
km² (0.39 sq miles)

- None
- Fewer than 1
- Up to 100
- More than 100

Towns and cities

Anywhere where a group of people live is called a settlement. A village is a small settlement, a town is bigger, and the largest kind is a city. The capital city of a country is where its government is based. About half the people in the world live in a town or a city.

Lines on maps

To make it easy to measure distances and find places on a map, the Earth is divided up with imaginary lines. The two sets of lines are called longitude and latitude. They are numbered in degrees (°) and minutes (′).

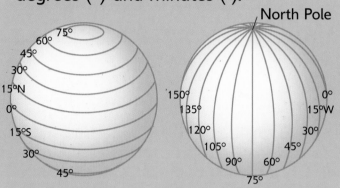

Lines of latitude run around the globe. On maps they usually run from left to right.

Longitude lines run from the North to the South Pole, and usually from top to bottom on maps.

This drawing of the Earth shows the North Pole and the main lines of longitude and latitude.

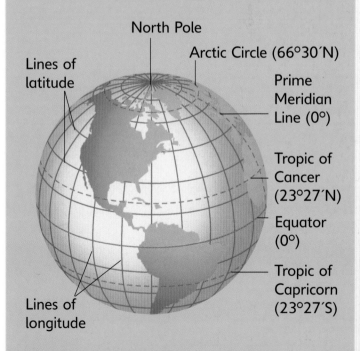

This globe is tipped slightly forward so the North Pole shows. This means that you can't quite see the South Pole.

The world's land

This is a physical map. It shows the different kinds of land in each continent.

The top half of the globe is called the northern hemisphere.

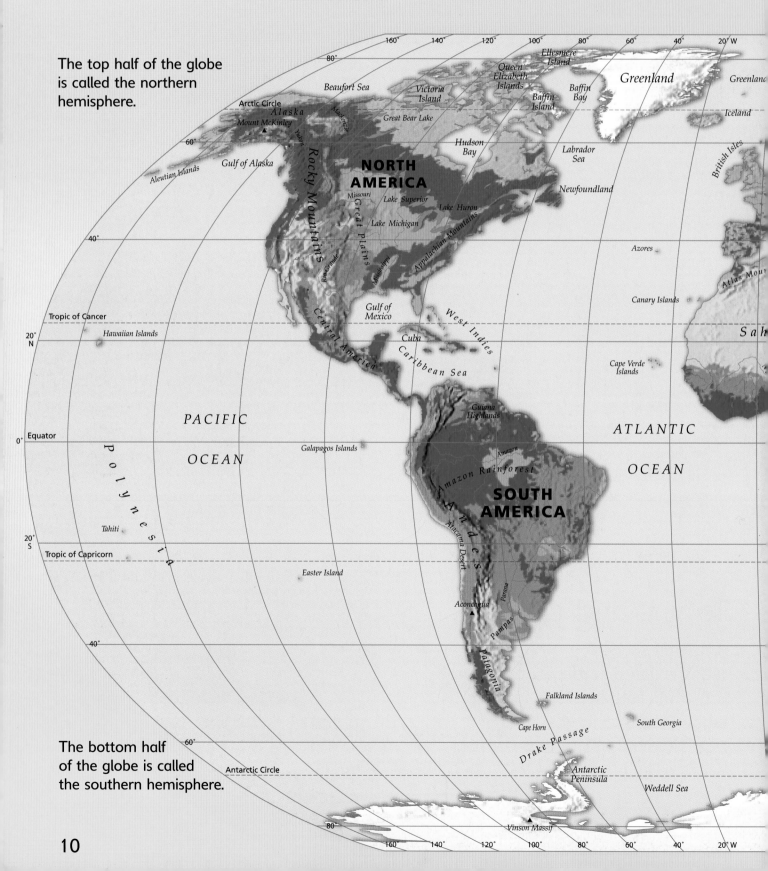

The bottom half of the globe is called the southern hemisphere.

Key to map of the world's land

- Forest
- Grassland
- Desert
- Mountain (only high mountains are shown)
- Tundra (frozen ground with no trees)
- Ice (areas where the ice or snow never melts)
- Crops (land used for growing plants for people and animals to eat)
- Sea
- Lake or inland sea
- River
- ▲ Mountain peak

Scale

| 0km | 3,000km |
| 0 miles | 1,860 miles |

ARCTIC OCEAN

Svalbard
North Cape
Novaya Zemlya
Barents Sea
Kara Sea
Severnaya Zemlya
Laptev Sea
New Siberia Islands
East Siberian Sea
Arctic Circle

candinavia
EUROPE
Danube
Black Sea
Mount Elbrus ▲
Volga
Caspian Sea
Ural Mountains
Ob
Yenisey
Siberia
Lena
Verkhoyansk Range
Bering Sea
Kamchatka Peninsula
Sea of Okhotsk
Amur

Mediterranean Sea
Libyan Desert
Nile
Arabia
Aral Sea
Altai Mountains
Lake Baikal
A S I A
Gobi Desert
Yellow
Sea of Japan
Japan
Honshu

Desert
Red Sea
Rub al Khali (Empty Quarter)
Indus
Himalayas
Ganges
Mount Everest ▲
Yangtze
China
East China Sea
PACIFIC
Tropic of Cancer

hel
Arabian Sea
India
Bay of Bengal
Mekong
Taiwan
Luzon
Philippines
Micronesia
OCEAN

Ethiopian Highlands
Cape Comorin
Sri Lanka
South China Sea
Mindanao

AFRICA
Lake Victoria
Kilimanjaro ▲
Seychelles
Sumatra
Borneo
Celebes
Java Sea
New Guinea
Mount Wilhelm ▲
Solomon Islands
Melanesia
Equator

Congo
Comoro Islands
INDIAN
Java
Arafura Sea
Fiji Islands

Zambezi
Madagascar
OCEAN
Mauritius
Coral Sea
New Caledonia
20° S

Namib Desert
Great Sandy Desert
O C E A N I A
Tropic of Capricorn

Great Victoria Desert
Great Barrier Reef
Great Dividing Range

Cape of Good Hope
Tasman Sea
North Island
New Zealand
40°

Kerguelen Islands
Tasmania
South Island

60°

SOUTHERN OCEAN
Antarctic Circle

A N T A R C T I C A
Ross Sea
80°

20° E   40°   60°   80°   100°   120°   140°   160°   180°

Countries of the world

This is a political map. It shows the different countries that make up each continent. Can you find your country on the map?

North America

This continent includes three huge countries – Canada, the USA and Mexico. It also includes the Caribbean islands and the countries in the strip of land that joins onto South America.

Key to North America map
- ■ Capital city
- ○ Major city or town
- — Border (where one country joins another one)
- — River
- ▨ Coast

PACIFIC OCEAN

Scale
0km	1,000km
0 miles	620 miles

Raccoons live in North and Central America. They usually sleep in trees during the day and come out at night to feed.

Internet links

For links to websites with quizzes on North America and maps to print, go to **www.usborne-quicklinks.com**

ARCTIC OCEAN

Queen Elizabeth Islands

Arctic Circle

Bering Strait

Point Barrow

Beaufort Sea

Parry Island

Bering Sea

Yukon

ALASKA (U.S.A.)

Mount McKinley ▲

○ Anchorage

Victoria Island

Gulf of Alaska

Mackenzie

Great Bear Lake

R O C K Y

Great Slave Lake

C A N A D

Lake Athabasca

Reindeer Lake

Vancouver

M O U N T A I N S

○ Calgary

G r e a t

Winnip

○ Seattle

Columbia

Missouri

P l a i n s

Great Salt Lake

San Francisco ○

C a l i f o r n i a

U N I T E D   S T A T E S

○ Denver

(U S A

Colorado

Los Angeles ○

Phoenix ○

Ciudad Juarez ○

T e x

L o w e r   C a l i f o r n i a

Rio Gran

Hermosillo ○

Monterrey ○

Tropic of Cancer

MEXIC

■ Guadalajar

■ Mexico City

○ Acapulco

Hawaiian Islands (U.S.A.)

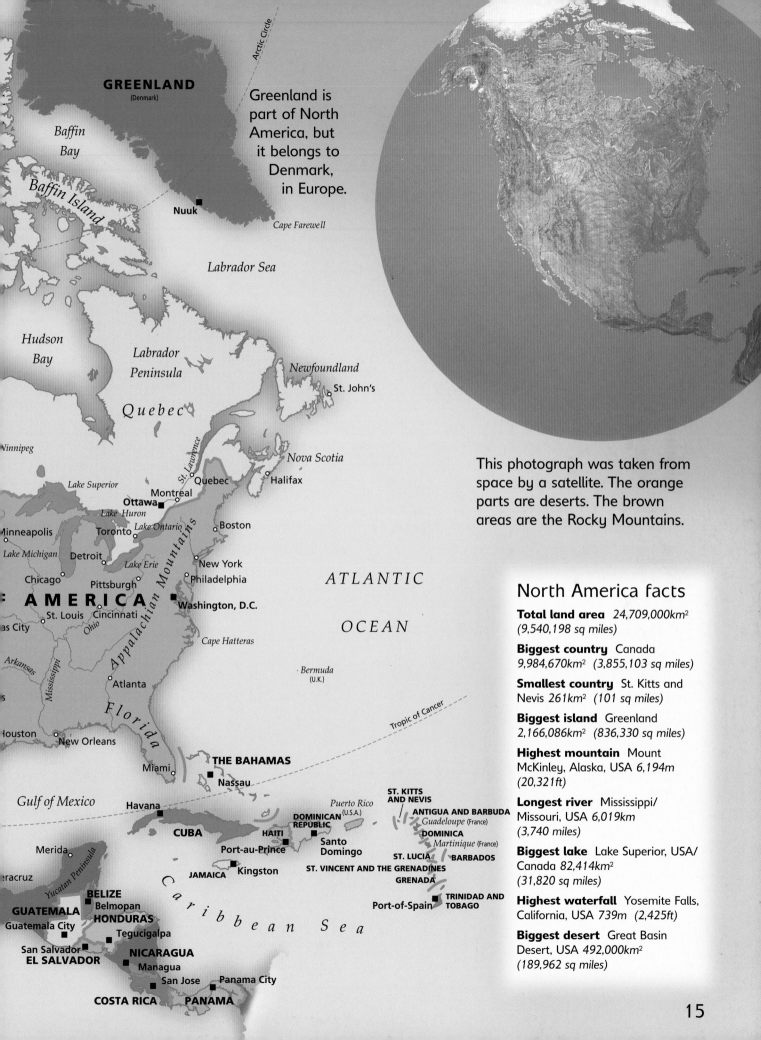

GREENLAND
(Denmark)

Baffin Bay

Baffin Island

Nuuk

Greenland is part of North America, but it belongs to Denmark, in Europe.

Cape Farewell

Labrador Sea

Hudson Bay

Labrador Peninsula

Newfoundland

Quebec

St. John's

Winnipeg

St. Lawrence

Quebec

Nova Scotia

Lake Superior

Montreal

Halifax

Ottawa

Lake Huron

Minneapolis

Toronto

Lake Ontario

Boston

Lake Michigan

Detroit

Lake Erie

New York

Chicago

Pittsburgh

Philadelphia

A M E R I C A

St. Louis

Cincinnati

Ohio

Washington, D.C.

as City

Appalachian Mountains

Arkansas

Mississippi

Atlanta

Cape Hatteras

Florida

Houston

New Orleans

Miami

ATLANTIC OCEAN

Bermuda (U.K.)

This photograph was taken from space by a satellite. The orange parts are deserts. The brown areas are the Rocky Mountains.

Tropic of Cancer

THE BAHAMAS

Nassau

Gulf of Mexico

Havana

Puerto Rico (U.S.A.)

ST. KITTS AND NEVIS

CUBA

DOMINICAN REPUBLIC

ANTIGUA AND BARBUDA

Guadeloupe (France)

Merida

HAITI

Port-au-Prince

Santo Domingo

DOMINICA

Martinique (France)

eracruz

ST. LUCIA

Yucatan Peninsula

JAMAICA

Kingston

ST. VINCENT AND THE GRENADINES

BARBADOS

GRENADA

BELIZE

Belmopan

Caribbean Sea

TRINIDAD AND TOBAGO

GUATEMALA

HONDURAS

Port-of-Spain

Guatemala City

Tegucigalpa

San Salvador

NICARAGUA

EL SALVADOR

Managua

San Jose

Panama City

COSTA RICA

PANAMA

North America facts

Total land area *24,709,000km² (9,540,198 sq miles)*

Biggest country Canada *9,984,670km² (3,855,103 sq miles)*

Smallest country St. Kitts and Nevis *261km² (101 sq miles)*

Biggest island Greenland *2,166,086km² (836,330 sq miles)*

Highest mountain Mount McKinley, Alaska, USA *6,194m (20,321ft)*

Longest river Mississippi/ Missouri, USA *6,019km (3,740 miles)*

Biggest lake Lake Superior, USA/ Canada *82,414km² (31,820 sq miles)*

Highest waterfall Yosemite Falls, California, USA *739m (2,425ft)*

Biggest desert Great Basin Desert, USA *492,000km² (189,962 sq miles)*

15

Using the land

Much of the land in North America is hard to live and work on. Some areas are hot and rocky, and some are freezing and snowy. In other parts of North America, the land and weather are just right for farming.

Shapes in the rock

In the southwest USA, some of the rocky land has slowly been worn away by rivers to make channels called canyons. Strong winds and rain have worn the rock away even more, making strange, rippling shapes.

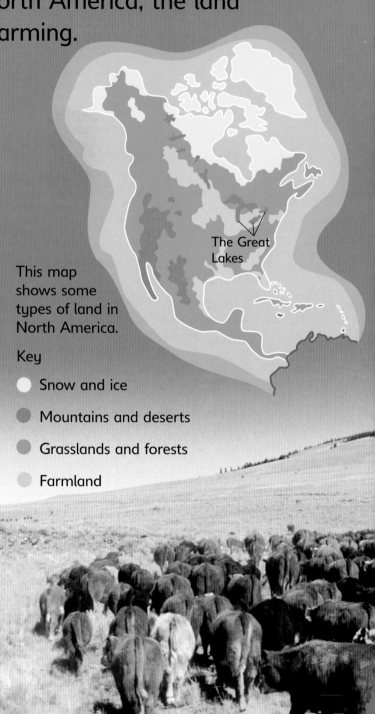

This map shows some types of land in North America.

Key

● Snow and ice

● Mountains and deserts

● Grasslands and forests

● Farmland

The Great Lakes

This strange photograph shows part of a small canyon in Arizona. The orange rock is called sandstone and the big cat is a puma.

16

Shaking ground

The Earth's crust is made up of huge slabs of rock, called plates. Sometimes they push or slide against each other, making the ground shake. This is called an earthquake. The San Andreas Fault, in the west of the USA, is a place where two plates slide past each other. Earthquakes often happen there.

This house fell down after a big earthquake in San Francisco, a city on the San Andreas Fault.

Massive farms

In the USA, Canada and Mexico, there are many huge cattle farms, called ranches. The cattle are farmed for their meat and skins. Other farms in North America grow crops such as corn and vegetables in enormous fields.

Internet links

For links to websites where you can explore the Grand Canyon and other American landscapes, go to **www.usborne-quicklinks.com**

One of the best ways for cowboys to move around their land and round up cattle is on horseback. Some farms are so big it would take days to walk across them.

17

Cities and celebrations

Explorers from Europe arrived in North America a few hundred years ago. But people have lived there for many thousands of years. Today, people come from all over the world to live there.

Stone cities

The Maya and the Aztec people lived in Mexico before European settlers came. The Maya built beautiful cities and pyramid-shaped temples out of stone. Ruins of these can still be seen today, on the Yucatan Peninsula in Mexico.

This map shows where some early North American people lived.

Key

- Aztecs
- Maya
- Native American tribes

Inuit
Inuit
Chipewyan
Cree
Inuit
Cree
Blackfoot
Chippewa
Huron
Chinook
Crow
Cheyenne
Cherokee
Comanche
Sioux
Iroquois
Hopi
Chickshaw
Navajo
Creek
Chocktaw
Apache
Yucatan Peninsula

This Mayan temple is over 1,000 years old.

The Maya believed their kings were gods and built temples like this one to worship them.

Busy city

New York City is the biggest city in the USA, and also one of the largest cities in the world. Over 8 million people live there, and thousands more visit every year.

Internet links

For links to websites where you can take virtual tours of North American cities and explore ancient sites, go to **www.usborne-quicklinks.com**

Part of New York is on an island called Manhattan. Bridges join Manhattan to the rest of the city.

Icy homeland

Inuit people live in the icy north of Canada, in an area called Nunavut. It's too cold to grow crops there, so Inuit hunters catch animals and fish for people to eat.

This boy has just caught a fish while ice fishing. He cut a hole in the frozen lake to fish through.

Calypso music

People visit the Caribbean islands for warm weather and sandy beaches. The islands are also famous for calypso music, which people play on drums made out of old oil cans.

This girl is dressed for Trinidad's carnival. Dancing and music are an important part of the celebrations.

South America

South America stretches down from the equator almost as far as the Antarctic. It is joined to North America by a narrow strip of land at the edge of Colombia.

Key to South America map

- ■ Capital city
- ○ Major city or town
- ▨ Border (where one country joins another one)
- — River
- ▨ Coast

Scale

0km	1,000km
0 miles	620 miles

Caribbean Sea

Maracaibo Caracas

VENEZUELA

Medellin
Bogota

Cali **COLOMBIA**

Guiana Highla...

Orinoco

Equator

Galapagos Islands (Ecuador)

Negro

Quito
ECUADOR
Guayaquil

Amazon

Amazon Rainfores...

PERU

Ucayali

A N D E S

Lima

Lake Titicaca **BOLIVIA**
La Paz

Atacama Desert

Sucre

Tropic of Capricorn

CHILE

San Migu... de Tucun...

A N D E S

PACIFIC

OCEAN

Aconcagua ▲ Cordoba

Rosa...

Santiago

ARGENTINA

Pamp...

Patagonia

Strait of Magella...

Tierra del Fueg...

Cape Horn

Drake Pass...

This is a toucan. Toucans live in South American rainforests. They use their long beaks to pick and eat fruit from the trees.

Map Labels

Georgetown
Paramaribo
ANA
Cayenne
URINAME
FRENCH GUIANA
(France)

ATLANTIC

OCEAN

na Reservoir *Amazon*
Belem

Equator

Xingu
aus

Fortaleza

Tucurui Reservoir

B R A Z I L

Sobradinho Reservoir

Recife

Tocantins

Plateau of Mato Grosso

São Francisco

Brazilian Highlands

Salvador

Brasilia

Goiania

Belo Horizonte

Parana

Furnas Reservoir

RAGUAY

Rio de Janeiro

São Paulo

Tropic of Capricorn

Asuncion

Curitiba

Porto Alegre

ATLANTIC

OCEAN

URUGUAY
Montevideo

uenos Aires

lkland Islands
(U.K.)

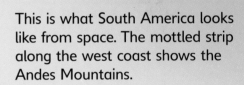

This is what South America looks like from space. The mottled strip along the west coast shows the Andes Mountains.

South America facts

Total land area 17,840,000km² (6,888,063 sq miles)

Biggest country Brazil 8,514,877km² (3,287,612 sq miles)

Smallest country Suriname 163,820km² (63,251 sq miles)

Biggest island Tierra del Fuego 47,401m² (18,302 sq miles)

Highest mountain Aconcagua, Argentina 6,962m (22,841ft)

Longest river Amazon, Brazil 6,800km (4,225 miles)

Biggest lake Lake Maracaibo, Venezuela 13,210km² (5,100 sq miles)

Highest waterfall Angel Falls, on the Churun River, Venezuela 979m (3,212ft)

Biggest desert Patagonian Desert, Argentina 670,000km² (258,688 sq miles)

Internet links

For links to websites with South America maps to print, go to **www.usborne-quicklinks.com**

Wettest and driest

South America has one of the wettest places on Earth in it – the Amazon Rainforest. But it also has the Atacama Desert, which is one of the driest. South America's Andes Mountains make up the the longest chain of mountains in the world.

Snowy peaks

The Andes Mountains are over 7,000km (4,300 miles) long, and stretch all the way down the continent. The lower slopes are good for farming, but the high peaks are snowy and bleak. More than 30 of the peaks in the Andes are volcanoes.

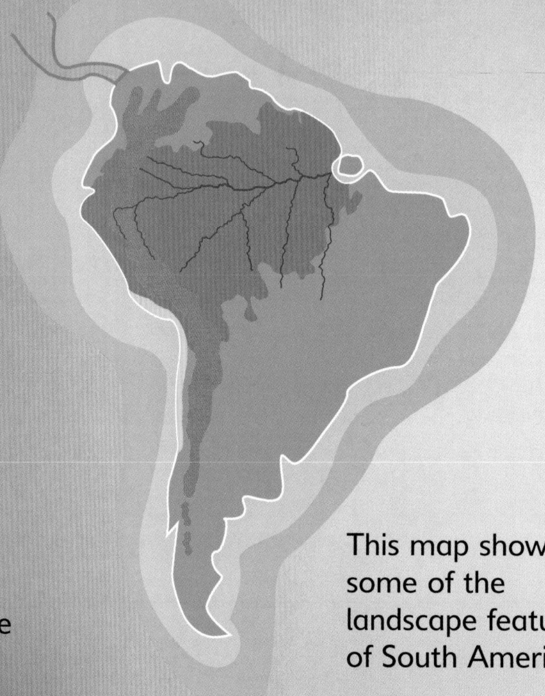

This map shows some of the landscape features of South America.

This climber is close to the top of Huascaran, one of the highest peaks in the Andes.

Forest homes

The Amazon Rainforest is the biggest rainforest in the world. It's always hot there and it rains nearly every day. The forest is home to a huge number of plants and animals.

This blue morpho butterfly comes from the Amazon. It's as big as a man's hand.

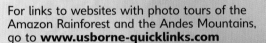

Internet links

For links to websites with photo tours of the Amazon Rainforest and the Andes Mountains, go to **www.usborne-quicklinks.com**

Dry ground

The Atacama Desert, in Chile, is next to the Pacific Ocean but it is the driest place on the planet. In some parts of the desert, people think it may never have rained at all.

Desert plants like these have long roots to reach way down into the cracked earth for water.

Mighty river

There's more water in the Amazon River than in any other river in the world. Over 1,000 smaller rivers flow into it, from all over the north part of South America. It is also one of the longest rivers, and winds nearly all the way across the top of the continent.

This boy is paddling his boat along the Amazon River. The main part of the river is so wide there are no bridges over it.

Places for living

South Americans live high in the mountains, deep in the rainforest, and even in the desert. Many people live in tiny farming villages, but South America also has some of the biggest cities in the world.

This map shows the places where most people live in South America.

Key
people in each km²
(0.39 sq miles)

None
Fewer than 1
Up to 100
More than 100

The Uros people use boats made of reeds to cross Lake Titicaca.

Mountain lake

Lake Titicaca is high up in the Andes Mountains, near Peru and Bolivia. The Uros people live by the lake and go fishing in its icy waters. Some of them live on floating islands made of reeds.

Mysterious statues

Easter Island, in the Pacific Ocean, is covered in hundreds of stone figures called *moai*. They were made by the first people who lived there, to worship their ancestors.

Most *moai* statues are at least twice the height of a man, and very heavy. How they were moved into place is a mystery.

City celebration

Early every year, the busy city of Rio de Janeiro in Brazil holds a carnival. It lasts for five days, with feasting, music and costume parades. Dancers take part in samba competitions across the city.

At carnival time in Rio de Janeiro, floats like this one carry costumed people through the streets of the city.

Internet links

For links to websites where you can learn more about South America, go to **www.usborne-quicklinks.com**

Asia

Asia is the biggest continent. It stretches from the Arctic Circle to the equator, and from the Ural Mountains in the west to the Pacific Ocean in the east.

The part of Russia on this side of the Ural Mountains is in Europe.

ARCTIC OCEAN

Novaya Zemlya
Barents Sea
Kara Sea
Arctic Circle
Norilsk
St. Petersburg
Arkhangelsk
Ural Mountains
Ob
Yenisey
S
Moscow
RUSS
Nizhniy Novgorod
Kazan
Yekaterinburg
Irtysh
Ob
Volga
Chelyabinsk
Omsk
Novosibirsk
Samara
Istanbul
Rostov
Aqtobe
Astana
Altai Mountains
Izmir
Ankara
Astrakhan
KAZAKHSTAN
Black Sea
Caucasus Mountains
Caspian Sea
Aral Sea
Lake Balkhash
TURKEY
GEORGIA
Tbilisi
Mediterranean Sea
Nicosia
ARMENIA
Yerevan
AZERBAIJAN
Urumqi
CYPRUS
Baku
UZBEKISTAN
Almaty
Beirut
SYRIA
Tabriz
TURKMENISTAN
Tashkent
Bishkek
LEBANON
Damascus
Ashgabat
KYRGYZSTAN
ISRAEL
Tehran
Dushanbe
Jerusalem
Amman
Baghdad
Mashhad
TAJIKISTAN
JORDAN
Euphrates
Tigris
Kunlun Mountain
IRAQ
IRAN
AFGHANISTAN
Plateau of Tibet
Syrian Desert
Basra
Kabul
Islamabad
HIMALAYAS
KUWAIT
Shiraz
Kandahar
Lhasa
Medina
SAUDI ARABIA
The Gulf
Indus
Delhi
Mount Everest
BAHRAIN
PAKISTAN
New Delhi
NEPAL
Jedda
QATAR
Kathmandu
Mecca
Riyadh
Abu Dhabi
Thar Desert
BHUTAN
UNITED ARAB EMIRATES
Muscat
Ganges
Rub al Khali
(Empty Quarter)
Karachi
Varanasi
BANGLADESH
Red Sea
OMAN
Nagpur
Dhaka
Sana
Mumbai (Bombay)
INDIA
Kolkata (Calcutta)
YEMEN
Arabian Sea
Bay of Bengal
Aden
Bangalore
Chennai (Madras)
Socotra (Yemen)
Cape Comorin
SRI LANKA
Colombo
Sri Jayewardenepura Kotte
MALDIVES
Male
Equator
INDIAN OCEAN

Key to Asia map

- ■ Capital city
- ○ Major city or town
- ▬ Border (where one country joins another one)
- ─ River
- ▓ Coast

Scale

0km	1,000km
0 miles	640 miles

Giant pandas live in bamboo forests in the high mountains of west China. These days, there are fewer than 2,500 giant pandas left in the wild.

Internet links

For links to websites with maps of Asia to print, go to **www.usborne-quicklinks.com**

East Siberian Sea

Laptev Sea

Bering Sea

Anadyr

Arctic Circle

Verkhoyansk Range

Lena

Okhotsk

Petropavlovsk-Kamchatskiy

Kamchatka Peninsula

Yakutsk

Sea of Okhotsk

ERIA

Lena

Komsomolsk

Amur

Hokkaido

Sapporo

Lake Baikal

Qiqihar

Sea of Japan

JAPAN

utsk

Ulan Bator

MONGOLIA

Shenyang

NORTH KOREA

Pyongyang

Tokyo

Seoul

Osaka

Honshu

bi Desert

Beijing

SOUTH KOREA

Hiroshima

Baotou

Xian

Yellow

CHINA

Shanghai

East China Sea

Tropic of Cancer

Hangzhou

Chongqing

Yangtze

Fuzhou

Taipei

Kunming

Taiwan (China)

PACIFIC

Xianggang (Hong Kong)

OCEAN

RMA NMAR)

Pyi Taw

LAOS

Hanoi

Hainan

Luzon

PHILIPPINES

Vientiane

goon

THAILAND

VIETNAM

South China Sea

Manila

Philippine Sea

angkok

CAMBODIA

Mekong

Phnom Penh

Ho Chi Minh City (Saigon)

Mindanao

Davao

Equator

BRUNEI

MALAYSIA

edan

Kuala Lumpur

Putrajaya

New Guinea

SINGAPORE

Borneo

Celebes

Palembang

INDONESIA

Banda Sea

Sumatra

Java Sea

Ujung Pandang

Arafura Sea

Jakarta

Surabaya

Dili

EAST TIMOR

Java

Timor Sea

The white ridges across the middle of this satellite photograph of Asia are the snowy peaks of mountain ranges.

Asia facts

Total land area
44,537,920km² (17,196,187 sq miles)

Biggest country Russia
Total area: 17,075,200km² (6,592,772 sq miles) Asiatic Russia: 12,780,800km² (4,934,694 sq miles)

Smallest country Maldives
300km² (116 sq miles)

Biggest island Borneo
748,168km² (288,869 sq miles)

Highest mountain Mount Everest, Nepal/China 8,848m (29,029ft)

Longest river Yangtze (Chang Jiang), China 6,380km (3,964 miles)

Biggest lake Caspian Sea, western Asia 370,999km² (143,244 sq miles)

Highest waterfall Jog Falls, India 253m (830ft)

Biggest desert Arabian Desert (deserts of Saudi Arabia) 2,330,000km² (900,000 sq miles)

All kinds of land

Asia has almost every kind of landscape you can think of. In the north, there are freezing forests. To the south, there are deserts and rainforests. Much of central Asia is covered in grassland.

Rice terraces

Some parts of Asia are very hilly. Farmers there make flat shelves called terraces in the land, to grow their crops on. The terraces stop water from running away down the slope, so the rice can grow. Many Asian farmers grow rice in this way.

These hillside terraces make flat areas for rice crops to grow.

High mountains

The highest mountains in the world are the Himalayas. They run through India, Nepal, Bhutan and China. The tallest peak is Mount Everest. Each year, many climbers try to reach the top.

This photograph shows the top, or summit, of Mount Everest. Strong winds are blowing snow off the top.

Rainy seasons

India has two main seasons. One is very rainy, and the other is very dry. These changing seasons are caused by the way the wind blows, and are called monsoons. The monsoons affect when crops can grow.

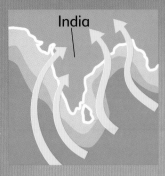

In winter, monsoon winds blow from the land out to sea. This is the dry season.

In summer, monsoon winds blow in from the sea, bringing rain. This is the wet season.

Great Wall of China

The people of China built an amazing wall hundreds of years ago, to protect their country from enemies. The Great Wall of China passes through deserts, mountains and grasslands along the northern edge of China.

Internet links

For links to websites with photographs of views of some amazing sights in Asia, go to **www.usborne-quicklinks.com**

The Great Wall of China is made of stone. These watch-towers helped soldiers see their enemies coming.

Many ways of life

Some areas of Asia have hardly any people living in them, but others are very crowded. People across Asia have lots of different beliefs and customs. Ancient traditions often survive alongside modern ways of life.

Tallest buildings

The Petronas Towers in Kuala Lumpur, the capital city of Malaysia are among the tallest buildings in the world. They are 452m (1,438ft) high, and have 88 floors, which are used for offices.

This market trader is taking fresh vegetables to sell at the floating market near Bangkok, in Thailand.

The Petronas Towers are much taller than other skyscrapers nearby.

Floating market

Every morning, small boats filled with fruit and vegetables form a floating market on a stretch of canal, near Bangkok in Thailand. Market traders paddle along the canal, selling food and souvenirs to local people and tourists.

Crowded country

China has the biggest population of any country. Over one-fifth of all the people in the world live there. Most of them live in big cities, though. In some parts of China, there are no people at all.

This map shows where most people live in China.

Internet links

For links to websites where you can find out about the everyday lives of people across Asia, go to **www.usborne-quicklinks.com**

Key
people in each km² (0.39 sq miles)

None (deserts)

Fewer than 1

Up to 100

More than 100

Glittering spires

Many of the world's religions started in Asia. Buddhism began in India and spread to other Asian countries, including Burma. There are many Buddhist temples in Burma. They are often decorated with pointed spires and large gold statues.

These golden spires are part of a Buddhist temple in Mandalay, Burma.

ATLANTIC

OCEAN

Mediterranean Sea

Madeira
(Portugal)

Oran Algiers   Tunis
Casablanca Rabat   TUNISIA
MOROCCO   Tripoli
Marrakech   Atlas Mountains   Benghazi

Canary Islands
(Spain)

ALGERIA   LIBYA

Laayoune

Tropic of Cancer   SAHARA DESER

WESTERN
SAHARA   Ahaggar
(Morocco)   Mountains

Tibesti
Mountains

MAURITANIA   MALI
Nouakchott   Tombouctou   NIGER
                        (Timbuktu)   CHAD
CAPE VERDE   Senegal   S a h e l   Lake Chad

Praia   Dakar   Niamey   Ndjamena
             SENEGAL   Bamako   Niger
THE GAMBIA   Banjul   Ouagadougou   Kano
             Bissau   BURKINA FASO
GUINEA-BISSAU   GUINEA   BENIN   NIGERIA
                                        TOGO
Conakry   Abuja   CENTR
SIERRA LEONE Freetown IVORY   Lake   Niger   AFRICA
              COAST   Volta   REPUBL
Monrovia   Yamoussoukro GHANA   Porto-Novo
LIBERIA   Accra   Lome   Lagos   CAMEROON   Bangui
                                          Malabo   Yaounde
                                    EQUATORIAL
Equator   GUINEA   Libreville CONGO
                              SAO TOME   GABON   Co
                              AND PRINCIPE
                                            Brazzaville
                                                    Kinshasa

Africa

Africa is the second
largest continent, and
the hottest. It stretches
from the Mediterranean
Sea in the north, across
the equator, and far
into the southern
hemisphere.

ATLANTIC

OCEAN   Luanda

                    Benguela   ANGOLA

Key to Africa map

■ Capital city
○ Major city or town
▬ Border (where one country
   joins another one)
── River
▨ Coast

NAMIBIA

Tropic of Capricorn Walvis Bay   Windho

                              Kalah
                              Dese

Internet links

For links to websites where
you can print out maps and
explore African countries, go to
www.usborne-quicklinks.com

Scale

0km   1,000km
0 miles   620 miles

                              Cape Town
                              Cape of Good Hope

The sandy brown areas on this satellite picture show how much of Africa is desert. The Sahara Desert is at the top of the continent.

Alexandria
Cairo
Suez
EGYPT
Nile
byan
desert
Jawf
Aswan
Lake Nasser
Tropic of Cancer

Red Sea
Port Sudan

Khartoum
ERITREA
Asmara
SUDAN
El Obeid
Blue Nile
White Nile
Lake Tana
DJIBOUTI
Djibouti
Ethiopian
Addis Ababa
Highlands
ETHIOPIA
SOMALIA
Juba
Lake Turkana
Kisangani
UGANDA
Kampala
KENYA
Equator
Mogadishu
Lake Victoria
Kigali
CONGO
Nairobi
RWANDA
MOCRATIC
Bujumbura
BURUNDI
Mwanza
Kilimanjaro
EPUBLIC)
Mombasa
Lake Tanganyika
Dodoma
Victoria
TANZANIA
Dar es Salaam
SEYCHELLES
INDIAN
Lubumbashi
COMOROS
Moroni
Lake Nyasa (Lake Malawi)
OCEAN
Ndola
ZAMBIA
Lilongwe
Lusaka
Zambezi
MALAWI
Lake Kariba
Nampula
Mozambique Channel
Harare
Toamasina
ZIMBABWE
MOZAMBIQUE
Antananarivo
MAURITIUS
Bulawayo
Beira
Port Louis
TSWANA
MADAGASCAR
Reunion (France)
borone
Pretoria (Tshwane)
Tropic of Capricorn
annesburg
Maputo
Mbabane
Lobamba
SWAZILAND
emfontein
Maseru
UTH
LESOTHO
Durban
ICA
Drakensberg
Port Elizabeth

Africa facts

Total land area 30,311,690km² *(11,703,409 sq miles)*

Biggest country Sudan 2,505,810km² *(967,499 sq miles)*

Smallest country Seychelles 455km² *(176 sq miles)*

Biggest island Madagascar 587,713km² *(226,917 sq miles)*

Highest mountain Kilimanjaro, Tanzania 5,895m *(19,241ft)*

Longest river River Nile, from Burundi to Egypt 6,671km *(4,145 miles)*

Biggest lake Lake Victoria, Tanzania 69,215km² *(26,724 miles)*

Highest waterfall Tugela Falls, South Africa 610m *(2,001ft)*

Biggest desert Sahara 9,100,000km² *(3,513,530 sq miles)*

This lion's sandy brown coat helps it blend in with its surroundings in its dry African grassland home.

Vast desert

A large part of Africa is covered by the Sahara, the biggest desert in the world. It's very hot there during the day, but at night the temperature often drops below freezing.

Dry desert

Hardly any rain falls in the Sahara Desert. The driest part is in Libya, where the desert is sandy. The wind blows the sand into huge piles called dunes, that form dramatic, curving shapes.

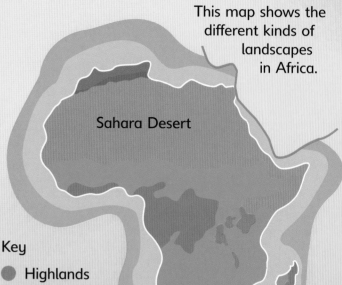

This map shows the different kinds of landscapes in Africa.

Sahara Desert

Key

● Highlands

● Scrub

● Desert

● Rainforest

● Savannah grasslands

Internet links

For links to websites about the different landscapes of Africa and the animals that live there, go to **www.usborne-quicklinks.com**

One of the best ways to cross the Sahara Desert is by camel. Camels can go a long time without water.

Thick rainforest

Some places in Africa have plenty of rain. The island of Madagascar is covered in thick, green rainforest. Many unusual animals, such as small, furry lemurs, live there.

Grassy plains

Large parts of Africa are hot grasslands called savannah. It's too dry there for many trees to grow, but there is enough rain for grasses. Savannah animals include lions, giraffes, elephants and zebras.

Ring-tailed lemurs live in the rainforests of Madagascar.

These zebras live in the savannah grasslands. The distant mountain is Kilimanjaro.

35

Farms and cities

Many people in Africa live in villages and work on farms. But now more and more people are moving to big cities to work and live.

This map shows the farming areas of Africa.

This is the Sahara Desert. No crops can grow here.

Thick rainforest

Key

 Farmland for crops and animals

Land not used for farming

This Zulu woman is carrying water in a clay pot.

Not enough water

Many parts of Africa don't get much rain. When there is too little rain, crops can't grow and people don't have enough water. This is called a drought. Sometimes, water may be carried or brought in pipes to a village where there is a drought.

Internet links

For links to websites about everyday life in different African countries, go to **www.usborne-quicklinks.com**

Farming for money

There are farms in most parts of Africa. Some grow grains such as corn or millet for people living nearby to eat. Others grow crops such as coffee or cocoa, to sell to other countries.

Selling crops is a good way for a country to make money. But it may mean that the people can't grow enough food to eat themselves.

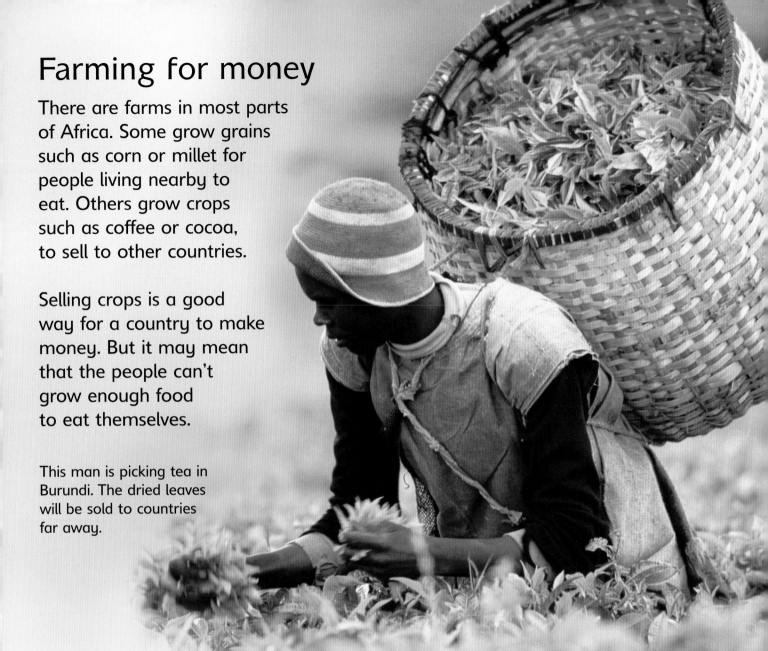

This man is picking tea in Burundi. The dried leaves will be sold to countries far away.

Growing city

Cape Town is one of the three capital cities of South Africa. It is built on flat land, close to the Atlantic Ocean, around the base of Table Mountain. Cape Town is a growing city. More and more people are moving there from the countryside to find better places to live and work.

This is Cape Town, in South Africa. The nearby mountain is covered in cloud.

37

Europe

Europe is a small continent, but it has many countries in it. Only the part of Russia west of the Ural Mountains is in Europe – the rest is in Asia.

Europe is home to many types of birds, such as this common European kingfisher.

ARCTIC OCEAN

Arctic Circle

Reykjavik
ICELAND

Norwegian Sea

ATLANTIC

OCEAN

Bay of Biscay

SWEDEN

Bergen
NORWAY
Oslo
Stockholm
Lake Vaner
Gothenburg

British Isles

Edinburgh
Belfast
IRELAND
Dublin
UNITED KINGDOM
Cardiff
London

North Sea

DENMARK
Copenhagen

Baltic Sea

Gdansk

Amsterdam
Hamburg
NETHERLANDS
The Hague
Brussels
BELGIUM
Berlin
GERMANY
Prague
POLAND

English Channel

Rhine
Elbe
Oder

LUXEMBOURG
Luxembourg

Seine

Paris

CZECH REPUBLIC

Nantes

Loire

Munich
Danube

Vienna
Bratislav
FRANCE
Ber n **LIECHTENSTEIN**
AUSTRIA
Budapest
Vaduz
SWITZERLAND
Lyon *The Alps*
SLOVENIA
Milan
Ljubljana
Zagreb
CROATIA
Turin
Po

Bordeaux

Bilbao

Oporto

PORTUGAL

Madrid
Lisbon
Tagus
SPAIN

Cordoba

Andorra la Vella
ANDORRA
MONACO
Marseille
SAN MARINO

Corsica (France)

ITALY
Rome **VATICAN CITY**
Naples

Sardinia (Italy)

Adriatic Sea

BOSNIA AND HERZEGOVINA
Sarajevo
MONTENEGR
Podgori
ALBA
Tiran

Barcelona
Valencia

Gibraltar (U.K.)

Mediterranean Sea

Sicily (Italy)

MALTA Valletta

Key to Europe map
- ■ Capital city
- ○ Major city or town
- ━ Border (where one country joins another one)
- ━ River
- ▬ Coast

Scale
0km	500km
0 miles	310 miles

North Cape

Barents Sea

pland

Murmansk

Kola Peninsula

Oulu

Pechora

Ukhta

FINLAND

Arkhangelsk

Northern Dvina

Ural Mountains

Arctic Circle

The rest of Russia is in Asia.

Lake Onega

R U S S I A

Perm

Lake Ladoga

sinki

St. Petersburg

Cherepovets

Rybinsk Reservoir

Volga

Kama

Tallinn

ESTONIA

Nizhniy Novgorod

Kazan

LATVIA

Riga

Moscow

Samara

LITHUANIA

Vilnius

Tula

SIA

Don

BELARUS

Minsk

Volga

saw

Voronezh

Vistula

ow

UKRAINE

Kiev

Kharkiv

Lviv

Dnieper

Volgograd

Volga

Dnipropetrovsk

Donetsk

Don

Astrakhan

VAKIA

Carpathian Mountains

MOLDOVA

Rostov

NGARY

Chisinau

Cluj-Napoca

Odesa

Sea of Azov

Caspian Sea

ROMANIA

Crimean Peninsula

grade

Bucharest

Caucasus Mountains

RBIA

Danube

Mount Elbrus

istina

BULGARIA

Black Sea

SOVO

Sofia

Skopje

ACEDONIA

REECE

Aegean Sea

Athens

This satellite photograph shows how Europe joins onto Asia. The big, white patch at the top is the ice that covers the Arctic.

Crete (Greece)

Europe facts

Total land area 10,180,000km² (3,930,520sq miles)

Biggest country Russia
Total area: 17,075,200km² (6,592,772 sq miles)
Area of European Russia: 4,294,400km² (1, 658,077 sq miles)

Smallest country Vatican City 0.44km² (0.17 sq miles)

Biggest island Great Britain 209,331km² (80,823 sq miles)

Highest mountain Mount Elbrus, Russia 5,642m (18,510ft)

Longest river Volga 3,692km (2,294 miles)

Biggest lake Lake Ladoga, Russia 17,700km² (6,834 sq miles)

Highest waterfall Utigard, on the Jostedal Glacier, Norway 800m (2,625ft)

Biggest desert There are no deserts in Europe.

Internet links

For links to websites where you can find maps to print and activities about Europe, go to **www.usborne-quicklinks.com**

Farms and hills

A lot of the land in Europe is gently hilly and good for farming. Some areas are rocky or snowy, and fewer crops grow there.

This map shows some of the crops that grow in Europe.

Key

- Grapes
- Olives (for oil)
- Fruit
- Potatoes
- Grains, such as wheat and barley

Europe

Asia

Mediterranean Sea

This market is in Rome, in Italy. Every day, people bring fresh fruit and vegetables from the farms nearby, to sell at the market.

Fruit and vegetables

The south of Europe is on the coast of the Mediterranean Sea. The weather there is very hot and dry in summer, but cool and wet in winter. Oranges, lemons and other citrus fruits grow well there, as well as many other kinds of fruit and vegetables.

Natural hot water

The island of Iceland has natural hot water, heated by rocks under the Earth. From time to time, jets of steam and hot water burst out through holes in the ground. These jets are called geysers.

This is Strokkur Geyser, in Iceland. Boiling hot water erupts from it every few minutes.

Jagged peaks

The largest group of mountains in Europe is the Alps. They formed millions of years ago, out of giant folds of rock. They have very jagged shapes, which were carved out by rivers of ice, called glaciers.

This picture shows how some of the valleys and lower slopes of the Alps are used for farming crops. Behind, you can see much higher, snowy peaks.

Internet links

For links to websites where you can discover the foods and traditions of European countries, go to **www.usborne-quicklinks.com**

Places to see

Europe is famous for its beautiful old cities and historic buildings. But many exciting modern buildings attract visitors too.

Eiffel Tower

The Eiffel Tower was built in 1889, in Paris, the capital city of France. Until 1930, it was the tallest tower in the world. Since it was built, more than 200 million people have visited it.

The Eiffel Tower in France is as tall as over 100 trucks stacked on top of each other.

Great cathedrals

Many cities in Europe have huge churches called cathedrals. They are made of carved stone, and took many years to build. Some have pointed spires on top, others have towers or rounded domes.

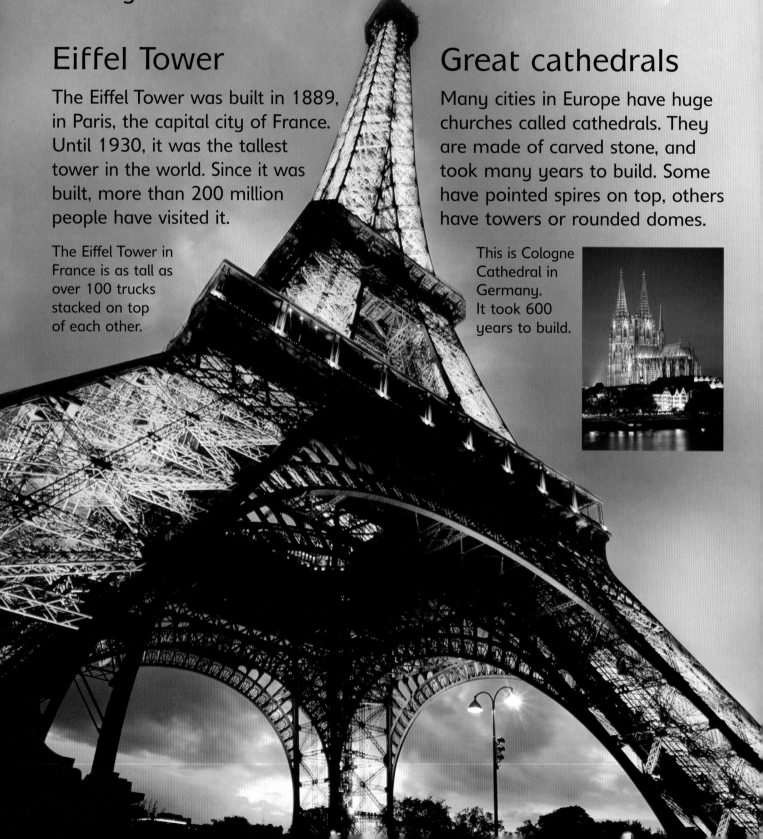

This is Cologne Cathedral in Germany. It took 600 years to build.

Modern buildings

There are some amazing modern buildings in Europe. One of the most interesting is Spain's Museo Guggenheim Bilbao. It is covered with huge curving sheets of metal.

This is the Museo Guggenheim Bilbao in Spain. It is a gallery where people go to look at modern art.

Roman remains

About 2,000 years ago, Rome was one of the biggest cities in the world. At that time, the Romans ruled all the lands around the Mediterranean Sea. Ruins of Roman buildings can still be seen in lots of places in Europe.

Internet links

For links to websites with virtual tours of Europe's historic buildings, go to **www.usborne-quicklinks.com**

This map shows where the Romans ruled in Europe. These lands were called the Roman Empire.

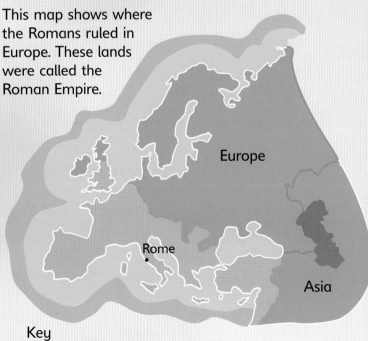

These are the remains of the Colosseum in Rome. People came here to see fighters called gladiators.

Key

● The Roman Empire

Oceania

Oceania is the smallest continent. It is made up of Australia, New Zealand and Papua New Guinea, as well as many smaller islands dotted across the Pacific Ocean.

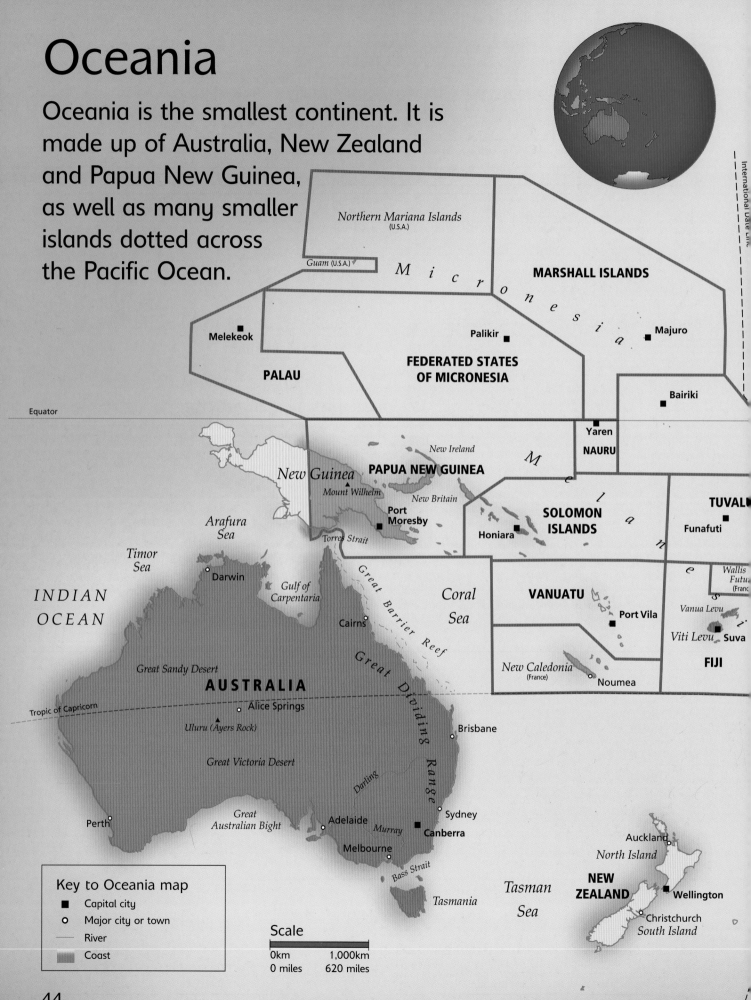

International Date Line

Northern Mariana Islands
(U.S.A.)

M i c r o n e s i a

Guam (U.S.A.)

MARSHALL ISLANDS

Melekeok ■

Palikir ■

Majuro ■

PALAU

**FEDERATED STATES
OF MICRONESIA**

Bairiki ■

Equator

Yaren ■
NAURU

New Ireland

M e

New Guinea
▲ *Mount Wilhelm*

PAPUA NEW GUINEA

New Britain

■ Port
Moresby

l

TUVALU

Funafuti ■

Torres Strait

**SOLOMON
ISLANDS**

Honiara ■

a

n

*Wallis
Futur*
(Franc

*Arafura
Sea*

Darwin ○

*Gulf of
Carpentaria*

Great Barrier Reef

*Coral
Sea*

VANUATU

Port Vila ■

e

s

Vanua Levu

*Timor
Sea*

*INDIAN
OCEAN*

Cairns ○

Viti Levu Suva ■

FIJI

New Caledonia
(France)

Noumea ○

Great Sandy Desert

AUSTRALIA

Tropic of Capricorn

Alice Springs ○

▲ *Uluru (Ayers Rock)*

Great Victoria Desert

Great Dividing Range

Brisbane ○

Darling

Perth ○

*Great
Australian Bight*

Adelaide ○

Murray

Sydney ○

■ **Canberra**

Auckland ○

Melbourne ○

Bass Strait

North Island

*Tasman
Sea*

**NEW
ZEALAND**

■ Wellington

Tasmania

Christchurch ○
South Island

Key to Oceania map
- ■ Capital city
- ○ Major city or town
- — River
- ▨ Coast

Scale

0km   1,000km
0 miles   620 miles

Oceania facts

Total land area 8,564,400km² (3,306,733 sq miles)

Biggest country Australia 7,741,220km² (2,988,902 sq miles)

Smallest country Nauru 21km² (8 sq miles)

Biggest island New Guinea 785,753km² (303,381 sq miles)

Highest mountain Mount Wilhelm, Papua New Guinea 4,509m (14,793ft)

Longest river Murray/Darling River Australia 3,718km (2,310 miles)

Biggest lake Lake Eyre, Australia 9,500km² (3,668 sq miles)

Highest waterfall Sutherland Falls on the Arthur River, New Zealand 580m (1,903ft)

Biggest desert Great Victoria Desert, Australia 388,500km² (150,001 sq miles)

PACIFIC OCEAN

Equator

P o l y n e s i a

KIRIBATI

Tokelau (New Zealand)

SAMOA
Apia

American Samoa (U.S.A.)

Cook Islands (New Zealand)

NGA
uaʻofa

Niue (New Zealand)

Tahiti

French Polynesia (France)

Tropic of Capricorn

International Date Line

Pitcairn Islands (U.K.)

Some of the countries in Oceania are made up of hundreds of islands, which are too small to be seen on this map. The red lines show where one country ends and another begins.

This photograph was taken from space. The light brown areas show that much of Australia is desert. The large, white area below Australia is Antarctica.

Wallabies live in the dry, dusty grasslands of Australia. Their long eyelashes protect their eyes from blowing sand.

Internet links

For links to websites with maps to print and video tours of countries in Oceania, go to **www.usborne-quicklinks.com**

Desert and ocean

Oceania is made up of over 20,000 islands in the Pacific Ocean. Most of them are tiny, but the desert land of Australia is huge. Many small islands are the tops of underwater volcanoes.

The deepest place

The bottom of the Pacific Ocean is covered in mountains, and valleys called trenches. The deepest place on Earth is in the Mariana Trench. It is over 11km (6.8 miles) deep. If you dropped a small rock into the sea, it would take over an hour to reach the bottom of the Mariana Trench.

These maps show the Mariana Trench and the Challenger Deep, which is its deepest part.

Japan (Asia)

Philippines (Asia)

Mariana Islands

Mariana Islands (enlarged)

Guam

Key

Islands

Trench

Challenger Deep

Ancient land

Most of Australia is a bare, rocky desert. Its land has hardly changed for millions of years. The rocks have slowly been worn into smooth shapes by the wind and rain.

Wave Rock in Australia looks like a towering wall of water. It was worn into this unusual shape by the wind and rain.

Internet links

For links to websites with photos and activities about Pacific islands, go to www.usborne-quicklinks.com

How islands form

The oldest islands in Oceania are made of limestone rock. The youngest islands are the tips of underwater volcanoes. These pictures show how an island forms and changes.

A volcano grows under the sea and rises up above the surface. When it stops erupting, animals and plants live on it.

Sea animals called corals grow around the edge of the dead volcano. They form a ring of coral called an atoll.

The coral dies and forms hard limestone. Forests grow on these new islands. The soft rock of the volcano is slowly worn away by the sea.

The middle part of this island in French Polynesia is a volcano. It is surrounded by coral reefs, which are large areas of tiny sea animals called corals.

Forests by the sea

Mangrove trees live on the edge of warm seas, with their roots partly underwater. Unlike most plants, they aren't harmed by salty sea water. Thick mangrove forests grow in Papua New Guinea and other islands in Oceania.

The roots of mangrove trees spread out wide and prop the trees up in the swampy ground.

Ocean living

Fewer people live in Oceania than on any other continent apart from Antarctica. Most of Oceania's people live near the sea.

Australia's people

Four out of five Australians live in towns and cities that are within one hour's drive of the sea. The rest live scattered across the huge desert area called the outback. People there live so far apart that some children have to do their schoolwork by mail or over the internet.

This map shows how many people live in different parts of Australia.

Most Australians live near the sea, and many enjoy water sports. This man has found a good wave to surf, near a beach in Australia.

Original people

Most people in Australia and New Zealand today are related to people who came from Europe. But the first people in Australia were the Aboriginal people, thousands of years before. The first settlers in New Zealand were the Maoris.

Key
people in each km² (0.39 sq miles)

- ● More than 50
- ● 4–50
- ● 2–4
- ● 1 – 2
- ● Fewer than 1

These men are wearing traditional Maori costumes. All children in New Zealand learn about Maori traditions at school.

Internet links

For links to websites about the Aboriginal people of Australia and the Maori of New Zealand, go to **www.usborne-quicklinks.com**

Fiji's farmers

Many Fijians are farmers. They grow enough food, such as corn and vegetables, for their families and other people in their villages. Some of their crops, such as coconuts and sugar cane, are sold to other countries.

Farming people on Fiji often live in one-room houses like these, with thatched roofs and woven floor mats inside.

Dressing up

The Huli people live in the mountains of Papua New Guinea. Huli men paint their faces and dress in spectacular feathered wigs to perform dances, which are famous all over the world.

This Huli man is putting on face paint. His wig is made from grasses, and feathers from a bird called a cassowary.

The Arctic

The area around the North Pole is called the Arctic. There's no land at the North Pole, but the sea there is so cold that its surface freezes and turns to thick ice.

The white patch on this globe shows the parts of the Arctic that are always covered with ice.

Frozen land

The Arctic Circle is an imaginary line around the Arctic. Eight countries have land inside the Arctic Circle. This land is called tundra. The soil there is frozen for most of the year. No trees can grow, but lichen and moss plants grow close to the ground.

Internet links

For links to websites where you can learn more about animals that live in the Arctic, go to **www.usborne-quicklinks.com**

Coping with cold

Arctic animals have to survive freezing temperatures. Many have thick, bushy white coats to keep them warm and help them blend in with the snow. Some have a layer of fat for extra warmth.

This baby harp seal has thick fur, and a layer of fat under its skin to keep it warm.

Scale

0km   1,000km
0 miles   620 miles

PACIFIC

OCEAN

JAPAN

○ Sapporo

Aleutian Islands

Bering
Sea

○ Petropavlosk-
Kamchatskiy

○ Anadyr

Arctic Circle

RUSSIA

ALASKA
(U.S.A.)

Chukchi
Sea

○ Anchorage

Rocky Mountains

Yukon

Wrangel
Island

East
Siberian
Sea

Verkhoyansk Range

Lena

Beaufort
Sea

New
Siberia
Islands

○ Yellowknife

Laptev
Sea

Yenisey

Victoria
Island

Queen
Elizabeth
Islands

Severnaya
Zemlya

North
Magnetic Pole
+

ARCTIC

CANADA

+ North Pole

OCEAN

Ellesmere
Island

Kara
Sea

Ob

Baffin
Island

Franz
Josef
Land

Ural Mountains

○ Yekaterinburg

Baffin
Bay

Novaya
Zemlya

RUSSIA

Davis Strait

GREENLAND
(Denmark)

Svalbard
(Norway)

Barents
Sea

■ **Nuuk**

Greenland
Sea

○ Murmansk

○ Arkhangelsk

Norwegian
Sea

Arctic Circle

○ Nizhniy
Novgorod

Reykjavik ■

FINLAND

■ **Helsinki**

■ Moscow

Key to Arctic map

■ Capital city

○ Major city or town

─── Border (where one country
joins another one)

─── River

███ Coast

ICELAND

Faroe
Islands
(Denmark)

SWEDEN

NORWAY

Oslo ○ ■ **Stockholm**

ESTONIA

LATVIA

ATLANTIC

North
Sea

OCEAN

DENMARK

Baltic
Sea

LITHUANIA

RUSSIA

BELARUS

IRELAND

UNITED
KINGDOM

GERMANY

POLAND

UKRAINE

NETHERLANDS

MOLDOVA

BELGIUM

CZECH
REPUBLIC

SLOVAKIA

Black Sea

The Antarctic

The Antarctic, also called Antarctica, is the continent at the South Pole. It is the coldest and windiest continent. The land is covered with ice over 2,000m (6,500ft) thick. Nine-tenths of all the world's ice is in the Antarctic.

The Antarctic is at the bottom of the Earth. It is surrounded by the Southern Ocean.

This scientist is studying an ice cave. The cave is in an ice shelf, about 100m (328ft) thick, that floats on the sea.

Home for scientists

People started exploring the Antarctic just over 100 years ago. The only people who live there today are scientists. They study the weather, ice and rocks to try to find out more about life on Earth.

Keeping warm

The Antarctic is home to thousands of penguins. They have layers of fat underneath their feathers to protect them from the cold, and huddle together in big groups for extra warmth. Penguins take turns standing at the edge of the group, where it's windy and much colder.

Internet links

For links to websites about life in the Antarctic, with video clips and satellite views, go to **www.usborne-quicklinks.com**

South Georgia
(U.K.)

South Sandwich
Islands
(U.K.)

Antarctic Circle

South Orkney Islands
(U.K.)

South Shetland Islands
(U.K.)

*Weddell
Sea*

Queen Maud Land

Coats
Land

Enderby
Land

*Antarctic
Peninsula*

ANTARCTICA

*East
Antarctica*

*Ronne
Ice Shelf*

*Bellingshausen
Sea*

Vinson Massif
▲
**5,140m
(16,863ft)**

Transantarctic Mountains

+ South Pole

*Ellsworth
Land*

*West
Antarctica*

*Amundsen
Sea*

Marie Byrd Land

*Ross
Ice Shelf*

Wilkes Land

Ross Sea

*Victoria
Land*

South Magnetic
Pole
+

Antarctic Circle

SOUTHERN
OCEAN

Scale

0km	1,000km
0 miles	620 miles

Key to Antarctic map

▲ Mountain

▢ Coast

This emperor penguin chick is
keeping warm by standing on
its mother's feet and snuggling
up against her tummy.

Flags of the world

North America

 Antigua and Barbuda

 Bahamas

 Barbados

 Belize

 Canada

 Costa Rica

 Cuba

 Dominica

 Dominican Republic

 El Salvador

 Grenada

 Guatemala

 Haiti

 Honduras

 Jamaica

 Mexico

 Nicaragua

 Panama

 St. Kitts and Nevis

 St. Lucia

 St. Vincent and the Grenadines

 Trinidad and Tobago

United States of America

South America

 Argentina

 Bolivia

 Brazil

 Chile

 Colombia

 Ecuador

 Guyana

 Paraguay

 Peru

 Suriname

Uruguay

Venezuela

Asia

 Afghanistan

 Armenia

 Azerbaijan

 Bahrain

 Bangladesh

 Bhutan

Brunei

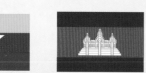 Burma (Myanmar)

 Cambodia

 China

East Timor

Georgia

Asia (continued)

 India

 Indonesia

 Iran

 Iraq

 Israel

 Japan

 Jordan

 Kazakhstan

 Kuwait

 Kyrgyzstan

 Laos

 Lebanon

 Malaysia

 Maldives

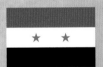 Mongolia

 Nepal

 North Korea

 Oman

 Pakistan

 Philippines

 Qatar

 Russian Federation

 Saudi Arabia

 Singapore

 South Korea

 Sri Lanka

 Syria

 Tajikistan

 Thailand

 Turkey

 Turkmenistan

 United Arab Emirates

 Uzbekistan

 Vietnam

 Yemen

Africa

 Algeria

 Angola

 Benin

 Botswana

 Burkina Faso

 Burundi

 Cameroon

 Cape Verde

 Central African Republic

 Chad

 Comoros

 Congo

 Congo (Democratic Republic)

 Djibouti

Egypt

Equatorial Guinea

Eritrea

Ethiopia

Africa (continued)

 Gabon

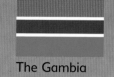 The Gambia

 Ghana

 Guinea

 Guinea-Bissau

 Ivory Coast

 Kenya

 Lesotho

 Liberia

Libya

 Madagascar

 Malawi

 Mali

 Mauritania

 Mauritius

 Morocco

 Mozambique

Namibia

 Niger

 Nigeria

 Rwanda

 Sao Tome and Principe

 Senegal

Seychelles

 Sierra Leone

 Somalia

 South Africa

 Sudan

 Swaziland

Tanzania

 Togo

 Tunisia

 Uganda

 Zambia

 Zimbabwe

Europe

 Albania

 Andorra

 Austria

Belarus

Belgium

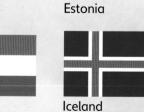 Bosnia and Herzegovina

Bulgaria

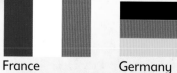 Croatia

 Cyprus

Czech Republic

Denmark

Estonia

Finland

France

Germany

Greece

Hungary

Iceland

56

Europe (continued)

 Ireland

 Italy

 Kosovo

 Latvia

 Liechtenstein

 Lithuania

 Luxembourg

 Macedonia

 Malta

 Moldova

 Monaco

 Montenegro

 Netherlands

 Norway

 Poland

 Portugal

 Romania

 Russian Federation

 San Marino

 Serbia

 Slovakia

 Slovenia

 Spain

 Sweden

 Switzerland

 Turkey

 Ukraine

 United Kingdom

 Vatican City

Oceania

 Australia

 Federated States of Micronesia

 Fiji

 Kiribati

 Marshall Islands

 Nauru

 New Zealand

 Palau

 Papau New Guinea

 Samoa

Solomon Islands

Tonga

Tuvalu

Vanuatu

Changing flags

Flags of the world change frequently. New flags are invented as new countries are born, or their situation changes.

For example, in 1991, there were important changes to the way South Africa was run. All adults in the country were allowed to vote in free elections for the first time. To celebrate this, a new flag was designed.

South African flag until 1994

South African flag from 1994

Internet links

For links to websites with flags and facts, go to
www.usborne-quicklinks.com

Map index

This is an index of all the places and features named on the maps. Each entry may contain the following parts: the name of the country, place or feature (in **bold** type), the country or region where a place or feature is (in *italic* type), and the page(s) where it can be found (in plain type). Some names also have a description explaining exactly what kind of place they are, for example, capital cities or rivers.

61

Index

Acknowledgements

This edition updated by Lisa Jane Gillespie and Vanessa Winch

Additional design: Adam Constantine, Michael Hill, Karen Tomlins, Joanne Kirkby, Luke Sargent and Lindsay North

Additional illustrations: Adam Larkum   Website adviser: Lisa Watts   American editor: Carrie Armstrong

Every effort has been made to trace the copyright holders of the material in this book. If any rights have been omitted, the publishers offer to rectify this in any future edition, following notification. The publishers are grateful to the following organizations and individuals for their contribution and permission to reproduce this material.

Cover Science Photo Library (tl) Louise Murray; (bl) Mike Agliolo; (br) Gary Hincks; **1** Science Photo Library/NASA; **2-3** Getty Images/Pal Hermansen; **5** Getty Images/Walter Bibikow; **7** Getty Images/Louise Murray; **8**(b) Dave G. Houser/CORBIS; **14**(bl) Digital Vision; **15**(tr) Julian Baum & David Angus/Science Photo Library; **16**(l) Getty Images/ John Giustina; **16-17** Getty Images/Macduff Everton; **17**(tr) Roger Ressmeyer/CORBIS; **18** Powerstock; **19**(tr) Owaki-Kulla/CORBIS, (bl) Friedrich Stark/Alamy, (br) Getty Images/Doug Armand; **20**(bl) Digital Vision; **21**(tr) Julian Baum & David Angus/Science Photo Library; **22** Galen Rowell/CORBIS; **23**(tl) Powerstock, (r) Owen Franken/ CORBIS, (bl) Robert Harding Picture Library Ltd/Alamy; **24** Jim Zuckerman/Alamy; **25**(r) Robert Harding Picture Library Ltd/Alamy, (l) Getty Images/Ary Diesendruck; **26**(bl) Digital Vision; **27**(tr) Julian Baum & David Angus/ Science Photo Library; **28**(l) Jon Arnold Images/Alamy, (br) Michael S. Lewis/CORBIS; **29** Miles Ertman/Masterfile; **30**(main) World Pictures, (bl) Macduff Everton/CORBIS; **31**(br) Powerstock; **33**(tr) Tom Van Sant/Geosphere Project, Santa Monica/Science Photo Library, (br) Digital Vision; **34-35**(b) Getty Images/Frans Lemmens; **35**(tr) Getty Images/Nick Garbutt, (m) NHPA/Daryl Balfour; **36** Dallas and John Heaton/Alamy; **37**(tr) Getty Images/Bruno De Hogues, (bl) Getty Images/Stephen Beer; **38**(ml) Digital Vision; **39**(br) Julian Baum & David Angus/Science Photo Library; **40**(bl) Art Kowalsky/Alamy; **40-41**(main) Jon Arnold Images/Alamy; **41**(mr) Getty Images/Wilfried Krecichwost; **42**(main) Getty Images/John Lawrence, (mr) Getty Images/Jorg Greuel; **43**(t) Powerstock, (bl) Getty Images/A & L Sinibaldi; **45**(t) Planetary Visions Ltd/Science Photo Library, (b) Digital Vision; **46**(b) Jean Paul Ferrero/Ardea London Ltd; **47**(t) Chad Ehlers/Alamy, (br) Theo Allofs/CORBIS; **48**(t) Mark A. Johnson/CORBIS, (br) Anders Ryman/CORBIS; **49**(ml) Jon Arnold Images/Alamy, (r) Wolfgang Kaehler/CORBIS; **50**(b) W. Perry Conway/ CORBIS; **52** Graham Neden, Ecoscene/CORBIS; **53**(br) Tim David/CORBIS.